MW00424680

TREASURES OF THE MASTER WITHIN

A SPIRITUAL JOURNEY

TREASURES OF
THE MASTER WITHIN

White Eagle's sayings from
THE LIGHT BRINGER

THE WHITE EAGLE PUBLISHING TRUST

NEW LANDS · LISS · HAMPSHIRE · ENGLAND

First published October 2002

© The White Eagle Publishing Trust, 2002

British Library Cataloguing-in-Publication Data

A Catalogue record for this book
is available from the British Library

ISBN 0-85487-142-X

'The Light Bringer' was first published in May 2001

Set in Arepo at the Publisher
and printed and bound in Great Britain at
the University Press, Cambridge

CONTENTS

V

INTRODUCTION

THIS IS a traveller's guide. It offers a journey that demonstrates the progressive unfoldment of the spirit, and it seeks to provide hope, encouragement and wisdom for the path. Readers of an earlier White Eagle book, THE QUIET MIND, may find that it leads on from that, but TREASURES OF THE LIGHT BRINGER is complete in itself.

The sayings are all (bar one or two) extracted from White Eagle's recent book THE LIGHT BRINGER. That book is largely about the Master for the new age and what form he or she will take. THE LIGHT BRINGER is a mystical book, very much centred upon the figure of St John, upon whose 'ray' White Eagle says he works. Here is one of the statements White Eagle makes about St John, one which has inspired the present book.

Jesus came to teach the people how to live the life on the physical plane within their communities. But John began to teach people the purpose of Jesus' teaching, because it is only when men and women can live the life of love and brotherhood towards each other that they can then begin to develop those soul powers of which we speak, those heavenly powers with which God the heavenly Father–Mother has endowed them.

The sayings in TREASURES OF THE MASTER WITHIN, however, are directly to do with the path the individual takes, preparing for revelation of the beauty that lies ahead. This is the respect in which the book is one to be carried at all times, whether the path be sweet or bitter.

It takes its shape from some words IN THE LIGHT BRINGER which might well have made a saying themselves:

Through a long, long journey each soul has also been learning, training, gaining power to send forth the light from every one of the seven sacred centres in its own body, and to draw upon the seven sacred planetary forces which work through each sign of the zodiac. Perfected man–woman not only sees that blazing Star at his or her initiation, but realizes that he or she in truth is that Star.

TREASURES OF THE MASTER WITHIN tells the story of a journey from the isolation of unawakened consciousness into what White Eagle would call universal (or Star) consciousness. Although the Star White Eagle so often talks of is a six-pointed one, that Star has a seventh point at its heart, and the number seven recurs again and again in the symbolism of the book. It might relate to the Great Rays, of which there are seven, for instance; but more importantly, the plan of the book follows a loose 'seven ages' principle. That conventionally means from birth to death, but in this case it is from birth to enlightenment. The first chapter is additionally to do with the birth of the new age. The second chapter is about suffering, which often is the prompt for us to take up a spiritual path. The third is about healing, both of the individual and of the world through the developing concept of brotherhood (see p. xi), which is symbolized by the six-pointed Star. In the fourth chapter we are experiencing the path towards complete healing, not only for individuals, but for all. The fifth is concerned with the development of soul gifts, particularly intuition. In the sixth, we are given a glimpse of what self-mastery truly is. The last is about realization, but in the Boddhisatva (Buddhist) sense. In other words, it is a realization that cannot be fully had until all creation is raised into the light.

There is another aspect to the sevenfold system in the book, in that the chapters link with the seven principal chakras. The chakras are suggested by the ornament at the head of each chapter as well as in the italicized words there. The chapter ornament is derived from the traditional Hindu diagram for the chakra, with a different number of petals for each. Although each chapter is only loosely tied to its chakra, reading the chapter will subtly help in understanding the role of the chakra in human development. Because White Eagle, in THE LIGHT BRINGER, specifically links these chakras to a planetary ray (see the quotation on p. viii), we have included the appropriate planet in these headnotes as well. In the case of the brow and crown, we have suggested Uranus and Neptune individually, although White Eagle ascribes the two planets to the head centres generally.

The Star symbol is amplified in the book but also in these words about the chakras:

The pivot of all these centres in the evolved type of person is the heart, which is like the sun of your universe. The heart centre breathes in and it breathes out. It absorbs—it takes in—sunlight. As the physical sun sustains life in the body, so the spiritual light and warmth behind that sun sustains the spiritual life in each individual.

Conceive the colours emitted by the chakras as very clear, bright, and pure; in the centre is a Sstar of white, representing the blending of all the colours into the one ray of white, indicative of the great light.

The title, 'Treasure of the Master Within', reminds us of the source of any truth that is real. It is not White Eagle, the author, who is the Master. Who then *is* White Eagle? Just a wise teacher, speaking through the medium Grace

Cooke. As we have seen, he works on the ray of St John, but in the teaching in this book one can feel that not only are the Christian saints and sages close by, but also familiar figures from other traditions: Buddha, Avalokitesvara, representing compassion (in Chinese, Guanyin); Shiva, creator and destroyer; Krishna. He also conjures up, even in these extracts, a very powerful sense of the great Mother.

He reminds us too of the great cycle of the heavens by which we are entering the Aquarian age. Above all he speaks as one of the Brotherhood of the Star beyond the veil. This is more than just a brotherhood of men and of women; it is a brotherhood behind life, representing all life: all levels of life, all forms and manifestations of life.

In a few cases the extracts have been very lightly edited so as to be complete in their new context. The words 'brotherhood' and 'master' have to be regarded as fully inclusive of both sexes; they do not permit acceptable alternative expressions. White Eagle normally regards brotherhood as a quality embracing all life, not just the human.

The lotus designs are by Liz Elmhirst.

JCH

FIRST CHAPTER

Incarnation and the New Age
Muladhara (root) chakra; Mars and the Moon

Y ou cannot comprehend infinity, nor eternity, but you can listen when we tell you that deep, deep within you, in the inner planes of consciousness, are worlds of indescribable and unbelievable perfection; and that, as you

13

learn to command yourself, your emotions, your fears, your anxieties—as you learn to enter into the sanctuary of peace in preparation—you will, by your own freewill and power, advance into the glories of a world perfect in colour, harmony; a world of music, a world of goodness, a world where everything falls into its appointed place without hindrance.

MANY beautiful qualities in human nature are going to be brought forth in the new age. Life will become longer, because as each person evolves he or she will touch divine wisdom.

KEEP calm, simple and humble, and give from your hearts the truest brotherhood you understand, and you will assist not in revolution, but in steady, progressive evolution.

Men and women will walk and talk with angels, but remember that it takes an angel to recognize an angel, a god to recognize a god, so until men and women have developed the necessary qualities within themselves, they remain unconscious of the presence of angels or of gods.

❶

TRAIN yourself to behold beauty in many forms. See the beauty in the light of another's face, the beauty of love in the eyes of a child, the beauty of love and light in the eyes and in the face of a very old person. Look always for that light, that beauty.

Know that the world is not going to remain in its present state of chaos.

❖

WE DO not speak of a life divorced from this earth when we tell you of a life of beauty, of glory, of perfection; a life of happiness, harmony and beauty. We speak of the life which you can first of all realize within your own being, and secondly on the outermost plane. Heaven can indeed be realized on earth.

❖

YOU have been told there is to be a second coming of Christ, the Lord of this earth planet. When is this to be? There is ample evidence that the time draws near, and this is shown particularly in the soul-preparation of many whom you encounter. There is aspiration in you. The Christ above and the Christ within alike are raising you to meet Him–Her on that higher plane of consciousness, when the Christ comes in all power and glory.

YOU are looking forward to the second coming of Christ, for it is said so clearly that Christ would come again; but we have said on many occasions that this second coming will be in the heart of every man and woman. It will be the awakening of the light in them.

A *new heaven and a new earth.* The new heaven is in you yourself. You have within your soul the power to rise up into the higher realms of life and light, and enter into the glories of the heaven world in full consciousness.

YOU will find in every quarter that the most unexpected men and women will be demonstrating to the world that they are the instruments of the spirit. Look for the secret key, look for the figure carrying the water pot [the sign of Aquarius], look for the person in your everyday life who is being quickened in spirit.

KEEP on the lookout for the quickening of the spirit in earthly people, and especially in so-called worldly people; because often the worldly people are the people of experience and great humanity. They know and understand the temptations and the pains and the suffering of human life.

HUMANITY makes progress: it does not regress, and every method used to bring about its birth into the spiritual life is necessary. Look out upon the world as it is with tolerance and love and hope.

TRY TO think of the brotherhood in spirit as a brotherhood of souls. You will find that all are just brethren, with no thought of gender.

We would have you realize that you have within yourself a centre of light and power. Within you lies the opportunity to grow in spirit, to grow in stature, until you, too, become as the Master.

A WORLD teacher is one through whom the light shines without being obscured. The great Light can shine through any human vehicle.

MASTERS do not blazon their qualities or advertise themselves. *Seek and ye shall find; knock and the door shall be opened unto you!*

❶

YOU have always existed, because you are a seed of the infinite eternal Spirit; and when you understand the governing laws of life—and that every action, every word and every thought is impressed upon finer ethers, an impression which is there for all time—then you will realize how it is that the future can be foretold.

HOPE

There are planes of life undreamt-of by you, you who are imprisoned in earthiness. But this does not mean that comprehension of these glories in the heavens cannot be realized while you are living in the physical body.

WE GIVE you hope. You are marching forward. Earth's humanity has awakened, and slowly, almost imperceptibly, humanity responds and raises itself, even as a child stirs in the womb.

THE GREAT thing in the new age is going to be a parallel development of the human and the divine nature; the human being and the divine being. In the age into which you are advancing, there will be great stimulation of both the materiality and the spirituality of the human race. Religion will come from the heart and every one of you will learn to unfold your own God-qualities and God-powers.

YOUR only way is the way of the spirit. Do not lay aside spiritual things; you cannot live a life centred upon personal enjoyment while around you men and women are suffering. However obscure you feel yourself to be, you must be true to the spirit of Christ within.

A GREAT opportunity is now being presented to you—and to all humanity. You are the builders of the new age. It is not good for you to sit down complacently. For as surely as humanity (or the western world) settles down in complacency, there will arise in another part of the world a powerful force which will again challenge that complacency, and make humanity rise to the occasion and give true service to the vast human family.

DO NOT wrap your robes around you as the Pharisees did, but be filled with sympathy and understanding for humanity and humanity's need.

SECOND CHAPTER

*Suffering and its cure
Svadhisthana (sacral) chakra; Saturn*

BRINGING FORTH THE GOOD

Nothing is wasted in life: no experience whatsoever.

ACTIONS, words and thoughts, like seeds sown in the ground, unfailingly produce an effect. What that effect or outcome is, is no less than the future that awaits the soul. This is the true way of reading the future, for life is governed by a divine law which states that as the soul sows, it will surely reap. Your future, then, is stored in the present. As you think, speak and act today, so you are sowing the seeds for tomorrow's harvest.

PEOPLE are not born to suffer. We say that unreservedly. Each one of you was created to know joy and happiness. There is only one way in which joy and happiness can be attained, and that is by the way of spiritual realization. Such happiness is eternal; its duration is not for one life only.

WE want to make it perfectly clear that you your-self have the control key to your powerhouse.

THERE is nothing so important as God. God is omnipotent, all-power; God is omniscient, all-wise (the all-wise Mother aspect); and God is omnipresent, ever-present. God is in everyone, in every creature, in all nature. God is in the air you breathe. God is in every cell of your body. God is closer than breathing, nearer than hands and feet, because God and you are one—but you do not know it yet. You have not burst the bonds of the physical consciousness and do not realize that you are potentially yourself a God.

THE MOTHER aspect of God is dual and destroys as well as creates. Before the new age of Aquarius can fully be ushered in, there has to be a breaking-down of old conditions. We witness this breaking-down everywhere; but those hurt in the process need healing. Indeed, they must be healed in order to bring forth the new, beautiful age of the spirit.

WHEN a condition has served its purpose it must be absorbed, it must go, and this is the value of the destructive element in life. We would give you a true perspective of the value of destruction—of the clearing away of old

29

methods and old ideas, and of making ready for the coming of the good, the true and the beautiful. This is what we mean when we say that the balance must be maintained.

All your problems and difficulties, though very hard to bear at times, have a meaning and will prove worthwhile, because it is through enduring them with courage, faith and trust in the love and wisdom of your Creator that you will go forward towards the perfect state and the Golden City of God.

REMEMBER the trials and the difficulties in another person's life which may make them irritable and sharp. Turn away wrath by gentleness and love, remembering that as you feel hurt and irritated, so may your companions feel too. Remember that until you can feel with the feeling of your companions, you cannot be a master soul. Until each of you can love your neighbour, you cannot receive the wisdom of the gods.

BE WITHOUT fear. Surrender to God. Then you will be filled with love and light. You will help the world forward towards peace, and you will help all those who are in darkness because they are full of fear—even your so-called enemies.

Why is there such terrible suffering? Because humanity has starved itself of the Mother principle for many centuries. There has been domination, first by the body and then by the intellect or brain. Both have tended to imprison, if not slay, the divine Mother principle, which is wisdom and love.

WHEN the spirit of the Mother works hand in hand with the true Father principle (which is the higher, the divine mind), you will get a return to sanity, to harmony, to happiness. The feminine aspect, the divine Mother aspect, is the tenderness, the love and the gentleness in life without which spiritual death must ensue.

The human spirit can become so radiant, so dominant over the physical life, that it can penetrate to the higher realms of consciousness which you think of as heaven. Instead of this heavenly state being in some faraway sphere up in the clouds, this heaven can be found here on earth.

THE GREAT need you have at present is to understand that you have an inner spiritual life and an outer worldly life. It is essential that all of you begin to develop your spiritual part. You have pure spirit within your own being.

IT IS good to make a habit not of dreaming your way through life, but of becoming very conscious at all times of the divine will and divine presence in the heart.

THIS IS the secret: to live, to know and to be in the consciousness of the Infinite Love and Light, and to live for spirit and not for matter. Matter is secondary. Nothing matters more than this spiritual life in you. It is the key to heaven—heaven on earth, as well as the heaven world after death.

THERE IS BEAUTY BEHIND CHAOS AND HAPPINESS BEYOND PAIN

GREAT happiness, exceeding happiness, can be painful. Pain and joy are akin to each other, being two separate aspects of the same thing, being light and shade, both springing from the same principle. Through the human being undergoing pain, the soul goes through its formation, and is strengthened and built up. Once you know this you will not shrink from any experience.

OUT OF chaos, God creates beauty and perfection. You are the instrument of God and you can be and are being used to bring about a right state for all people.

WE WHO see a little deeper recognize a strange beauty beneath the sufferings of humanity. Behind every experience, every sorrow, every saddening, sordid thing, there is reason, a great purpose. Some day, somewhere, somehow you will know that there is no difference between intense sorrow and intense joy.

YOU CAN enter into the deepest depths of hell and there find God.

WHEN you suffer grievous pain and come up against harsh conditions, you are crucified. But will it help you if White Eagle tells you that when you are crucified you are very close to the great awakening, to the resurrection, when you will find greater beauty, and more satisfying, deeper happiness, than you have ever known before? So, when crucifixion comes into your life, whatever form it takes, remember that after crucifixion follows the resurrection, and after the resurrection follows the ascension.

The world is under the influence of Saturn at the present time, and in the same way that old Saturn is the guide which leads the individual to the altar of initiation, so Saturn will lead the nations to the altar of initiation—initiation into the great brotherhoods. Saturn is doing its work right well!

IT IS largely by suffering that humanity learns to listen to the elder brethren, who, from time to time, restate the simple truth. This truth consists of ways of service to relieve suffering. It consists of ways towards harmony and happiness, towards Christ, the ultimate goal of every soul.

THE LIGHT is gradually being born upon your earth plane. The second coming is stimulating the soul qualities in men and women. As they open their inner eyes to the world of light, so the whole vibration, the whole physical substance of the body will change and become pure, and will become as a master's body.

ALL THINGS are working together for good, and the man or woman who loves God must see how this is so. When things happen, do not

say in a foolish way, 'How terrible!'. Leave God
to know God's work, and God's great angels to
know their work, for they are always working
to put right the foolish mistakes of human kind.

CONTROL OF THE SELF

We know there is great eagerness in the
hearts of some of you to get on with the
work. You find life difficult sometimes, and feel
despairing about the world, and more especially
about yourselves. We of the Great Brotherhood
in spirit bring you power and love and wisdom
to help you.

❷

IF YOU find it difficult to restrain and control
yourself when you want to, at those moments
take a deep breath and say to yourself many
times: 'God is with me'. Then be still and let

All Good manifest through you. Unwanted thoughts cannot penetrate your aura if you have sent forth love from the temple, the centre in your heart.

WHEN YOU are distracted by material things, keep very calm, keep very still. Remember the Brethren of the Silence, whose very power of achievement lies in silence. Touch the silence, and the power of the spirit will flow into you and disperse all your fears.

A PERFECT CHANNEL FOR THE LIGHT

Jesus was a true psychic, in the highest sense, because his psyche, or soul, was perfected and poised. He was a perfect channel; a calm and beautiful sea upon which the light of the sun was reflected clearly and beautifully. He walked upon the sea: a demonstration, not of his miraculous powers over nature, but to teach those of his disciples with understanding that he was able to control the soul—that is, the emotions. He had risen above the turbulence of the desire-vehicles of life.

IT IS A very simple message, the one which Jesus left with his disciples—*love one another.*

THE KEY IS WITHIN

Some of you still find cause to misjudge others. Strive to overcome intolerance. Try to put yourself in another's place and feel what they feel during their crucifixion (because that is what it can amount to). Above all, keep your values right, your vision pure, your heart full of love.

YOU DO not really grasp that within you is something more precious, more beautiful, more wonderful than you have ever conceived.

AS THE bulb grows in the dark soil and eventually raises its head to the sunlight, a beautiful flower, so every human soul contains within its being potential qualities of becoming a master soul, a perfect jewel.

THE MASTER key that you have within you is the Christ, or the spiritual power of the divine will that is in everyone. If ever you are troubled by unwanted thoughts, remember: let the I AM take control. A master has complete control of circumstances through having gained mastery of his or her own being.

PROGRESS

Let all nations seek the divine will for the whole earth. No country need be anxious if it puts into operation the law of God in all its dealings. We know that many problems will arise, but we still maintain that the spiritual law is the way of peace.

THE SPIRIT, the seed-atom, sown in the heart chakra, is the seed of the Christ. You confront the conditions most necessary during your incarnations to develop that seed and bring forth a perfected soul, and a flowering of the Christ spirit.

THERE is no death! Progress, progress, progress … growth; a life-force ever moving onward, forward into the Sun. Hope!

THIRD CHAPTER

Healing
Manipuraka and Surya (solar
plexus) chakras; Jupiter

If you play your part, you will become an ever more pure and great channel for the mighty flood of the Christ love and light which is even now descending upon you all. For now, at this very moment, the Christ power is baptizing the earth, and wounds are being healed.

Healing is the intake into the body of the eternal Sun, the light. If you can call upon this light, if you can breathe it in, if you can live consciously in this light, it will actually control the cells of the physical body. The body is so heavy, material life so strong—but do not forget the power of God to recreate the living cells of your body.

WE SEE, shining above the great company of brethren in the heavens, the blazing Christ Star: the symbol of the Christ man or woman. The spiritual power descending into humanity is symbolized by the triangle with the point coming down and perfectly interpenetrating and balancing human nature. The human being is made perfect by the Christ birth, the greatest thing that can ever happen on this planet.

HEALING IS IN GIVING

SEEK for the gentle love of the lord Christ in your brothers and sisters; and if you cannot see it immediately, nonetheless by your own efforts to love them you will in time evoke in them a response. This is the law of brotherhood: to look for love, to give love in all your ways; to live purely and kindly, to treat Mother Earth with consideration and thoughtfulness, to respect all life and not to shed the blood of any creature; to give love and to help life to a higher and more beautiful form on the earth.

WHEN YOU pray and meditate to help your brethren on earth, do not think only of peace; give forth the Christ light. Light, the light which holds the balance: this is what works the magic. The great white light of Christ is the healer of all ills of body and of soul.

NO-ONE can find God through the intellect alone. Everyone has to go through a development of their soul, their feelings and their love first.

THE six-pointed Star is the symbol of the perfectly-balanced life. If you can think of yourself as being composed of countless millions of tiny six-pointed stars, you may begin to realize your power—no, not your own power, but the power of God within you.

We of the Brotherhood of the Star return to you for one purpose—in order to help you to awaken to the knowledge of spiritual life, and the brotherhood of all life.

THE AQUARIAN Age, we would say, is the age in which humanity becomes conscious of its real nature. Within the heart, through the sufferings and restrictions brought by the influence of Saturn, the password is sounded which flings wide the gateway into the age of Aquarius.

RIGHT now, your intuition is awakening and urging you to seek, seek, seek for the light.

THE VERY first thing is to get your values right. Do not be confused between what is called material and what is called spiritual, but endeavour to live in the awareness of the presence and the power of the invisible to help you and to help all human kind along the path of evolution.

THE ANSWER to every human problem lies in the divine mind. Until all human beings can rise above self and make contact with that divine mind, they will not receive the guidance for which they long.

Remember your thoughts; keep a check on them. You will gradually re-create your conditions, re-create your life.

LACK OF mental control is the greatest hindrance in the Master's service. Peace is the achievement of controlled and wisely-directed emotion. The razor's edge upon which the disciple has to walk is to develop feeling, but also to control it.

THE EMOTIONS are always symbolized by water. When water is turbulent, you get a false reflection. If the water is calm, clear and pure, you get perfect reflections from above.

THE BOAT of your soul rocks in a great storm. When the soul calls rightly the Master hears. In you rises the divine power which causes you to be still, to be tranquil. Be at peace. Your Master takes over control of your boat—which is your soul—and you become calm.

NO HARM WILL COME

You do not need to think of yourself. All you have to do is to live your days, love everything and everybody; just breathe love, live love, think love—and then attacks cannot penetrate

your armour. Darkness will not touch you if you
are radiating light.

NO HARM can break through when the Christ
is manifesting through you. In the degree that
you can call forth that mild, peaceful, tranquil
love in your heart towards life—not only to
people but towards life itself, so that you are
radiating love—you are encircling your aura
with a white shield which is impenetrable by
the world.

A POWER THAT COMES FROM WITHIN

The human body can be likened to a temple. Within this temple is an altar, on
which burns a bright, clear flame. In your medi-

tation seek this altar: try to imagine it, and bow your head in surrender before that altar flame within your own temple.

GOD HAS created man and woman, put them in a world of infinite promise, given them infinite possibilities within. Only you yourself can develop yourself, and nothing can hold anyone back from developing those infinite possibilities, since the Infinite Spirit is all love, truth, wisdom, gentleness and brotherliness towards all creatures.

WHERE TO LOOK FOR STRENGTH

Keep your feet on the earth, but lift your faces towards the heavens. The light which floods into you from on high will steady your feet and guide them in the right path.

IF YOU would understand your own creation, your own evolution, the life to which you go, the purpose you must follow, you must seek deeply within your own breast where truth abides; and so realize the spiritual life—the life invisible—which interpenetrates every form of matter. Seek, and find this life invisible to be the living word of God.

THE SIX-POINTED STAR

We draw your attention to the symbol of the Christ Star—built up, created, as a beautiful, blazing Star pulsating with light. The rays stream forth afar and the symbol is ever-living; its rays are continually going out, illumining the earth. What is the origin of this Star? Insofar as this particular manifestation is concerned, it is the result of a long period of God-thought, good thought, loving thought, constructive thought, which has been sent forth by those working on earth and in spirit. This concerted effort, this power which has been going out for so long, creates the Star form. It is, however, far more than a thought-form, and is being projected out over the world and into the invisible spheres which surround this planet.

THE STAR is not only a great cosmic power, it is also a tender, loving, guiding power; a protecting power in your own lives.

THE MASTER knows your fears and your sorrows, and you will receive the comfort, the guidance and the love that you need as you go to him or her, as you go into the Star.

WHEN YOU send out the light of the Star, do not merely force it out from your brow chakra. Open yourself in humility, sweetness and love to the Christos, to the one who is called Christ—the human being who is made perfect—the perfect Son or Sun of God. When you want to send out the light of the Star, try first to get that feeling of love in your heart. Jesus said so simply, 'Love one another'. So we love God. We raise our thoughts to the apex of the golden triangle and visualize there the glorious Star. We hold that Star—that point of light—and in that point of light, right in the centre of that perfect, geometrical, six-pointed Star, we may hold the image of anyone we desire to help. Or we may just hold the vision of the Star and see its rays shining forth.

SALVATION

In the new age, religion will take an entirely different form. It will be a religion which will help each man and woman to develop the God within him- or herself; and each of you will learn that the best way to stimulate this divine power within is through group work. A few will be drawn together. *Where two or three are gathered together in my name there will I be in their midst,* said Christ through the master Jesus. Religion will take the form of group work: in other words, its form will be that of true brotherhood of the spirit.

YOU ARE spirit; and as spirit, you are a daughter or a son of God. As a child of God you can claim your birthright—which is the power of the spirit within to free you from bondage in a material world.

DO YOU see the true meaning of Christ being the saviour of human kind? It is not the fact of a physical body being nailed to a wooden cross which saves humanity from its sins, but you yourself when you rise (or go within) to that supreme plane of consciousness where you contact the solar force: your solar self, the Christ.

GOLDEN heights are waiting for you, along with every other soul; but first you must cast out false values and recognize that the most important thing in life is the awakening of the spirit of God within your own heart.

IF YOU can surrender yourselves to the sweet and lovely Star radiance, you will find that your pathway will be one of light and happiness and gentle peace.

D o not allow yourselves to fear, because if you do you will be going over to the enemy. You can choose to allow God to enter and use you to love and succour your companion beings—or allow the 'devil' to come in to condemn and destroy. The true brother or sister recognizes that every poor, fallen soul contains a spark of God which needs fanning into life.

REMEMBER, it is not your will when a miracle is performed. It is God's power, it is God's will. Surrender to God's will in all things.

THE WAY to unlock the door of the kingdom, the heavenly mysteries, is by the way of meditation and love; and not by meditation alone, but by living in a simple, loving, caring way towards all creatures.

UNDERSTAND the importance of the daily meditation, the preparation for the day which sets you up in thinking before you speak and act, the importance of the control of the temper and emotions. Make it habitual to welcome and respond to thoughts of purity, gentleness, kindliness and goodwill.

NOT ONLY are you a vessel of light, even as a little lamp burning on the altar, but you may relight the lamp of your brother, your sister.

FOURTH CHAPTER

Setting out on the Path
Anahata (heart) chakra; Venus

SERVICE AMONG OTHERS

Love, gentleness, courtesy, never wearying in well-doing, always being ready to give help when help is called for: by these things the heart chakra opens and the light streams forth from the heart.

YOU HAVE come back to earth for a special purpose; you have come not only to develop your divine consciousness but also to pioneer the pathway which will become the path for all who will follow. You cannot help but develop your own character and divinity if you are truly serving others.

THE person who has the inner light takes that light wherever he or she goes.

IN THE new age each person will learn to worship in his or her own temple—that is, in the sacred place of the heart. People will not live by physical values only, but by the light of their own spirit, and their own spirit will show them how to behave towards their companions. The cathedral of the new age will be one raised out of people's lives.

At some point you will be faced with an unshakeable truth. You will come to a barrier across which you cannot move until you have mastered the lesson of brotherhood. You have to recognize and realize this, and become one with all life, through love.

YOU WHO fear for material needs, remember God's love is omnipotent. God knows! For you, we say, take courage; step forward on life's path like sons and daughters of God. God has prepared the sustenance, the food, the experience which you need on life's journey, so that you may grow and evolve.

NEVER look to the future and anticipate this, that, or the other. Live today, with God, and no future can hold for you any greater joy than is yours today. Many folk spend their days waiting for something to happen, for something to turn up. This is to live in fear, and we would help you to see the foolishness of this. Live today. Live and be at peace, and you have entered your kingdom of heaven.

ABOVE all, we would ask you to cast out all fear. If you persevere with this one small lesson for even just a few weeks, at the end of that time you will realize what a great step forward you have taken. Be without fear. Surrender to God.

You can only lastingly find God through life, through your feelings, through your soul, so that the soul becomes like a bridge between heaven and earth, bringing humanity back again to God. The soul is the bridge.

THE SIX-POINTED Star is the most beautiful symbol of the perfectly-balanced soul, the soul

69

whose head is in the heavens, whose faculties are quickened to receive the light from above, and whose feet are firmly planted upon the road of earth, which the soul traverses with one object in view—to find and give true happiness of the spirit.

FROM THE heart of Jesus flowed continually the radiation of a pure white magic. Any human heart can still receive this same radiation from the heart of the Christ, and if that heart keeps pure and joyous it can in turn radiate light and healing to all the world.

WHEN LOVE comes into the heart it causes an illumination. Where love has entered, a man or woman looks like a little torch. When love comes in entirety into the human family, there will be so many lights that the fog will disappear.

Y ou must develop your spiritual being surely, strongly and purposefully, every day of your life: first by the practice of meditation, and secondly through the continual practice of love in your daily life.

THE INTUITION can be developed in meditation, not through activity of the mind, but through quiet contemplation within the sanctuary of the heart.

DO GOOD to your own soul, not thinking unduly about yourself but abiding by wise laws of right living, right eating, right thinking. Create as far as you can pure and right conditions in your home and surroundings.

YOU WISH to work with God to create harmony, beauty and healthfulness, holiness and happiness, not only for yourself but for all human kind. It is this motive of creative love which gives power and life to your thoughts and prayers. This is the work of brotherhood.

YOU GO right to the mark. You are direct in all your dealings, but are also aware of any hurt

which your brother or sister may feel, and so
you are careful and tender in action and speech.

SOME SPIRITUAL QUALITIES

The master Jesus came representing both
the human and the divine being. Here was
the one who could enter into the sorrows and
joys of his brothers and sisters; here was the one
who found in the simple things his greatest joy;
here was the man who worked in the fields, not
like a beast of burden, but as a son of God, with
his face towards the sun; and whose joy was to
serve life, to serve God, to serve his brother–
sister.

THE VERY gentleness and meekness portrayed
in the four gospels brings to you a picture of

Christ. If you would meet Him face to face, strive in all ways to do and think as He would do and think. He would be gentle, loving and compassionate, and have humility.

BE BRAVE and keep on with courage, and keep before you the golden light towards which you are ever moving.

IN YOUR meditation, you are being taught how to bring the higher chakras to life: that is, how to open your consciousness to the pure, the spiritual level of life. This is the right way to unfold the inner faculties. The sixth sense, the intuition, functions from the heart centre. The safe way and the correct way for spiritual unfoldment is to work from the heart of love.

The way is very difficult to find; and, being found, very difficult to walk steadfastly. The only way to maintain a foothold and to progress is not by taking up this or that path, but by entering the chamber within: by praying, with all one's strength, to the wisdom of God. When light comes, it will be not the light of intellect alone, but a light which urges the soul to love all.

IT IS NOT only a few selected ones who attain mastership or Christhood. All the children of

God have their feet set upon the selfsame path. But the soul must first of all recognize that life is a vast brotherhood.

ONLY THROUGH deeper and deeper meditation will you reach a clearer understanding and picture of the future, and of the path which you are travelling. You will arrive at a more profound happiness as you grow to understand what you are doing, and where you are going.

AS YOU progress on your path, it will be clearly demonstrated to you that what you think you become.

The golden age ... will not be founded upon material and scientific achievement, but by the simple and gentle of heart.

DIVINE fire is within your very being, and as you raise your face to the sun, the rays of the sun stimulate this individual spark.

OCCASIONALLY you hear of a reflection or a manifestation of the glory of the Christ coming in flashes through great people, and of course through those whom you call masters. You see through them the radiance, the glory, the beauty of the divine life. You think to worship, but never to draw near to that Being. You worship from afar instead of taking hold of yourself and working to perfect your own character and your own soul, so that it becomes fitted for that same divine spirit to manifest through you to all creatures. This is the whole purpose of your life.

AS MEN and women open their inner eyes to the world of light, so the whole vibration, the whole physical substance of the body, will change and become pure, and will become as a master's body.

AS YOU WALK THE PATH

It is hoped that one day you will become so impregnated with the holiness and love of the Master that you will carry that gentleness and love out into the world. Is it asking too much?

WHILE each of you must develop your own lone path, you are never left alone. A paradox!

MISTAKES do not matter. In comparison with the greater and wiser ones, we all make mistakes. The inner voice comes from the heart of wisdom, and not from the self. Intuition comes like a flash, it is an inward knowing. The thing is to have courage to act on it; to be prepared for whatever it brings.

TO ACHIEVE what we have told you you can find, you must work steadily onward. And we tell you that if you can put into practice in your daily life one iota of what you hear or read, flowing through from us in words, you will do very well indeed!

A rose is the symbol of a human heart fragrant with love. You may not often see hearts like this, but we do. We see many human hearts open to us and can inhale the perfume of sweet human love.

WHEN your heart centre opens in love and kindness towards all creatures, it begins to grow and to expand, and can be seen by those with clear vision as a light radiating forth.

There is one truth which we should like to make very clear, and this is that there are no short cuts. There is a difference between speeding up evolution and taking a short cut to heaven. The first of these is possible—indeed, it is now presented to humankind—but the second is entirely outside the plan. You cannot take a short cut in life.

YOU WILL always be hearing from us: *keep on keeping on*. So many cannot do this. They go to sleep by the wayside. They get discouraged. They turn back. But the soul who perseveres and keeps on keeping on reaches the goal of spiritual liberation.

NOT a weary day is lost. You learn, you are creating the whole time, so that when you arrive at that plane of true harmony of soul, there opens a vista of ever-increasing loveliness. It is not for us to tell you at this juncture of what awaits every soul. Be of good cheer! Live, sounding in your heart a mantram, 'I am in the centre of my universe; I am the centre of God's life; all wisdom, love and power dwells in me'.

PEOPLE find it such a temptation—it is much easier to do—to go here, there, everywhere; going to all kinds of places: to the west, to the east, to the south, in search of a master! And all the time the Master is within, so close to them!

FIFTH CHAPTER

Developing Spiritual Qualities
Visuddha (throat) chakra; Mercury

YOU HAVE IT IN YOUR POWER TO LEARN

Y̶ou have it in your power, when you have learnt to control your senses and emotions, to rise above the limited consciousness of your physical life and go through into those higher planes; to enter into the finer ethers which in-

84

terpenetrate gross physical matter, and see the glory of God's plan of creation, which is beyond the capacity of the finite mind to understand.

※ 5 ※

IT IS NOT until the individual is released from the finite mind that he or she can understand eternity. Eternity is now.

※ 5 ※

THE SILENT voice, which successive initiations will enable you to hear, will say to you: 'Yes, I remember, I know; I do not fully remember even now, but I have a feeling'. Oh, how valuable are these feelings! The angels help human evolution through feeling.

Thought can do anything in the world. Thoughts of anger, fear and hate form the root of all suffering and of wars. Thought can also bring forth beauty and harmony, and brotherhood, and all else that men and women long for. We know that by seeing only good, by creating good, by positive thought, we can help to bring about that which is desirable and good.

WE KNOW that all things can be done with love; but if you do not get knowledge, love can be compared to the flower which has not opened. Strive for knowledge; strive for full consciousness and understanding of what you are doing in the higher planes.

The New Jerusalem is the soul made perfect, man–woman made perfect. Do not think that it is just a condition which awaits you thousands upon thousands of years hence. You can begin to understand this perfect life now.

✸ (5)

THE SOUL is led by the guide through many intricate ways, many dark passages—which is what you are going through now in your earth life. You do not know where your road leads, nor when you will turn the corner, nor what you will find round it. Human life is really a passage through which the being—man or woman—is being led by its guide, not only in one incarnation, but through many.

✺ 5

Those of you who are used to meditation will realize the possibilities of creative thought, God-thought, good thought. Perfect thought creates perfect form, and you will create a perfect life in time.

DEVELOP WITH DISCERNMENT

Although you do not realize it, you are surrounded at all times by a vast company of spirit beings. You possess certain vehicles or bodies through which you can make contact with the different planes. Humanity has for long concentrated upon the stimulation and development of intellect. The time has now come for you all to develop your sixth sense, which we call intuition. This sixth sense, or ray of light, is destined to open for you the secrets of nature, of creation, and all spiritual life and purpose.

⚙ 5

THE LIGHT which is generated by any of you during the course of your spiritual unfoldment is a very real and tangible thing. It radiates from every pupil who unfolds his or her inner gifts, and it really penetrates the soul of another. It is a very sacred power to be used with delicacy and discernment.

⚙ 5

TRAIN yourself to be tranquil in mind, to control the emotions and direct them wisely: not to repress them but to raise them onto a higher plane of love and service and kindness. Through the blending of the intellect and the emotions the spirit is touched, the intuition reached.

❀ 5 ❀

WHEN you have learned to hear the voice of intuition, your reason will not take primary place. Reason will have served its purpose in your life, and its domination will pass away. Out of reason will come intuition, or the divine intelligence of the God self.

❀ 5 ❀

DREAMS—as we in spirit very well know, so we can speak from experience—actually create external conditions. *Where there is no vision the people perish!* So hold to your dreams and keep on keeping on.

If you do what you can to purify your own physical atoms by right thinking, right speech, right action, right living, judging no-one for what they do but looking to yourself; if you follow these precepts, then imperceptibly you will find that your consciousness is raised, and will uncover a happiness of which you have not dreamed. You will know peace in your heart, joy beyond earthly comprehension, and a gracious and gentle power which will enable you to open the prison doors of your life.

WE WANT you to understand that spirituality is not something quiescent, but strong and powerful, finer than the matter of earth, finer than the vibration of earth. It is the substance of life.

⌗ 5 ⌗

GOD'S plan is to bring beauty. We will not say perfection, not in the limited sense in which the word is understood. To us there is no standing still; even with God. We do not see a perfected Being, completely finished and there for ever. We wonder at and worship a God ever-growing more beautiful, ever sending forth greater waves of life and light, expressing divine Self not only in this universe, but in universes yet unborn.

THE HUMAN CAN BE A REFLECTION OF THE DIVINE

The symbol of the white rose inspires pure love, divine love, within you. The white rose and the red rose are two symbols of life— the white rose being pure spirit, and the red rose being the spirit or human soul after it has passed through deep human experiences.

STANDING by a lake (in the world of spirit) and watching the reflection of goodness and beauty, you can see your own reflection, and see yourself in comparison with God and God's manifestation of truth.

DEVELOPMENT of the sunlight within your own being enables you to develop what is loosely called clairvoyance or clear vision. Clear vision means an inward knowing. When you have this you know the truth, you recognize the love which exists in your brethren. You also understand their soul-needs.

The coming of the age of Aquarius will certainly bring into prominence the Mother, or the woman aspect of life. In other words, it is indicative of the development of intuition, or increase of soul power among the people of the earth. The First Principle, being representative of the Father, or the Will, must be balanced by the Mother, or the Intuition.

THE SOUL is peace-loving; the soul yearns for beauty, harmony and perfection; the soul, being intuitive, can look into the future desiring to protect the race, not to destroy it.

THAT which the heart absorbs is truth.

94

The spirit life interpenetrates the physical and there is no 'here' and 'over there' in the way you think. There is no impenetrable barrier between matter and spirit, but an interpenetration.

✶ 5 ✶

PSYCHIC gifts are waiting to be uncovered in every soul, but every soul has to be trained and developed to the highest level so that the world they make contact with is the heaven world.

✶ 5 ✶

YOUR whole life is lived within a concentration of cosmic forces, and like a magnet you attract to yourself conditions and powers like those you have awakened in yourself.

❋

DO NOT LET the spiritual things be to you as fantasies. Let the spiritual truths become to you the realities of life.

❋

NEVER reach outwards to find spirit people. That is a strange thing for us to tell you. Always go inwards to the heart. It is not in the brain, not in the solar plexus, but in the heart that you will make this true contact.

FORWARD AND ONWARD

THE WORLD of tomorrow will be built up on the resolutions, aspirations and determinations of humanity today; and if that world is to be all that you hope for, then it can only come if you declare yourself strong in the spirit, and are strong in the light of the Cosmic Christ, which is both within and without you.

YOUR MASTER says to you: 'Cast out fear ... be unafraid ... be whole ... know no desire'. And again: 'Be sincere to this woman or this man'. If your master's ideal in your heart makes you unwilling to stoop to the low and the mean and the petty, particularly in the things unseen or unknown—if you can act always as though your master is by your side, and do what you feel would be your master's way—then you are nearing the meeting-place, and will meet him or her face to face on earth.

※

THE DISCIPLE leaves all earthly things—
mind, body, possessions, desires—to follow
God. Having reached this understanding, you
can safely rely upon your intuition.

※

FORWARD, forward, forward, gaining every
day in spiritual qualities and powers which will
be the most holy and blessed part of your life
and the lives of all men and women in the future!

SIXTH CHAPTER

Brotherhood
Ajna (brow) chakra; Uranus and the Sun

HOW TO KNOW THE MASTER

How will your master appear? Listen! Your master may speak to you through the lips of another, tonight or tomorrow.

YOU MUST seek your master. He or she will not run after you and reveal him- or herself. Your master will not say, 'Lo, I am your master; follow me!'. No: it is for you to find him or her and then to follow. It may take a long time, but you can certainly meet your master face to face in this day of life; and your master can also speak to you through some book. You may hear and see him or her in some glorious sunset, or great piece of music, or in a lovely poem; in the message of a bed of flowers or in a pine tree.

THOSE who recognize a master must already have a degree of mastership themselves.

IT IS at the higher mental level that you will in time come face to face with the Elder Brethren.

You have to train yourselves first of all through meditation. We put meditation first, for the reason that as you learn to meditate, you are learning to raise your consciousness above the astral plane to the higher mental. True meditation takes place on the higher mental plane, and as you practise meditation you become more and more able to fix your consciousness upon this plane and to distinguish it from the confusion of the astral.

THE TEMPLE OF THE GOLDEN FLOWER

It may help you to know how you, as a simple brother, or a simple sister, may hold communion with your master. All that your highest self creates in the human form, all that your highest self is capable of imagining your master to be like, you will fashion into his or her form in your mind; and thus his or her presence will become a reality to you.

◀6▶

THE ASPIRANT today is not concerned with the monastic or ascetic life of old. He or she is called to mingle with humanity; to mingle with and bring through, into the minds of those he or she meets, the light of the ages.

◀6▶

WHEN YOU have really gained mastery over the physical body, the nervous system and the thinking—so that in all ways you can create the condition that the divine will within you wishes to create—then you are able, when you sit in meditation, to build round you 'the temple of the Golden Flower', exquisitely formed of spiritual or celestial substance. In meditation you are fully open like a beautiful flower, like the thousand-petalled lotus of the crown chakra, or the many-petalled lotus of the heart chakra.

THE PEACEMAKERS

Intuition can evolve to such a degree it becomes knowledge, absolute and certain knowledge of the God-life. This power flows through the hands, through the eyes, through the aura of people who have unfolded it. Such brethren walk the world carrying with them healing power. They are the peacemakers. This is the ability to reach and enter that higher plane of consciousness at any time, in any condition of life.

◀❬6❭▶

THE LIGHT is not only something beautiful in your heart, but a reality which permeates the very flesh which clothes your soul. The light has to shine through matter and use it, control it, glorify it.

◀❬6❭▶

WHEN illumination comes there is only one way in which it is possible to live, and that is by spontaneous love, kindness, gentleness, not only to brother man, or to the sister of your spirit, but to all creation.

YOU ARE LIGHT

The kingdom of God shall come upon earth when you have discovered that within your own souls is the light of the spirit of Christ, the Christ light, which is the seed given to every one of you.

❰6❱

YOU ARE here to use physical matter, and not allow it to dominate you. You are here; you are light; and you have to shine out through the darkness. You have to use your physical life and raise it, to transmute the heavy atoms of the physical body. Within you lies the power to change the very atoms of your body, for the physical atoms are the spiritual atoms.

❰6❱

WHEN THE divine fire is brought into full operation so that all the chakras are active as God intended, then the whole body will be in a state of ascension. We mean by this that the whole body, although still of a physical nature, will be functioning on a much higher plane of consciousness than it is at present.

WE SPEAK with knowledge; we know of that which we have seen in the higher worlds. We know that nature, as you see it on earth, is not yet perfect; but with men and women working harmoniously with nature, there will come further unfoldment. We see indeed a beautiful earth!

THERE SHALL BE NO MORE DEATH

May you see the vision of the New Jerusalem that lies within your innermost being;

and then may your vision be externalized on earth, on all the planes of life!

◀6▶

THE RENDING of the veil, spoken of in your bible, is the intermingling of those higher or spiritual planes of life with the physical planes. Humankind will open its eyes to the glories of heaven. There will be no more separation.

◀6▶

IT IS TRUE, there is no death. When you have passed the great barrier, you will be amazed and say: 'But I did not feel anything! Am I dead? I feel exactly the same'. There is no difference, except you have taken off one dress and left it behind.

JOHN saw *a new heaven and a new earth*—the holy city—like a new and more perfect Jerusalem. God, the spirit, is the spiritual sun; the soul, the spiritual moon; and the street of the city is of gold, clear as glass. The initiate walks always the golden path, and has neither dross, nor shadow.

THE MASTER KNOWS YOU

Remember this: you will find your master first in the secret chamber within your own heart. But you must know the master within first; you must know him–her in this way before you can hope to recognize your master manifested in a physical body.

WE SEEK the master, our master! For this brief moment let us forget all else. *My master!* Say it to yourself; close your eyes and say, 'My master.'. Do you form a picture of your master, or do you find it easier to visualize some picture of Jesus Christ and accept Him as your master? Never mind which. It is sufficient that you have a master, and that you desire to know him–her. Your master knows you as no living soul on earth can know.

FACE TO FACE WITH THE SELF

All that you can create in your mind of a beautiful, loving, gentle, pure and perfect man–woman, will enable you to meet your true master on the higher planes of consciousness.

◆⟨6⟩◆

ALL SEEK the light, yet not before others is your light lit: not even disclosed to your nearest and dearest, but in the innermost sanctuary, with no veil between you and your real self.

◆⟨6⟩◆

IF YOU meet with what you call failure, do not despair and say, 'I am not there yet'. The very fact that you are trying shows you are at one level already there. If not, you would not be trying. The fact that you can create a longing and set your vision on an ideal shows that you are ready.

THE OPENING FLOWER

As you pray and meditate, as you kneel in devotion, you are causing the light to

quicken in the chakras in your being, and causing them to open like the lotus.

❮6❯

THE FLAME upon the altar which you see in
your meditation may take on the form of a rose
with a brilliant jewel of light shining at its centre. If you see this, remember that you are gazing upon your own heart chakra. Or, when you
see the form of a lotus with its many petals, remember that you are gazing upon yet another
of your own chakras.

PIONEERS

You are pioneers, working for the great day
when cosmic and solar consciousness will
be the gift or the realization of all peoples.

112

NONE CAN act only of or for themselves. They may pride themselves on isolation, but it is impossible to injure another without injuring the self. After initiation into awareness of the group existence, the responsibility of the soul becomes vastly greater.

WHEN THE Christ within all people is raised up, and they worship in spirit and in true action and in daily service, then in themselves they must be raised up.

REALIZE WHO YOU ARE

When the soul has acquired all the lessons necessary, when it has attained a degree of completeness, it puts forth a more complete presentation of itself. Then you are able to see and recognize a master, an adept, an initiate.

ONCE you feel adoration and worship for the Solar Logos, the only-begotten of the Father–Mother God, you feel also a stirring within. Now will come the rising of this solar force into your etheric body, into your physical body, into all your bodies and into every centre. These centres will begin to pulsate and will open as a flower opens to the sunlight. You will be able to recognize yourself as a true yogi. Do not think that the term means someone who walks around with a begging bowl. A yogi is one who has attained union with God-consciousness.

SEVENTH CHAPTER

Illumination
Sahasrara (crown) chakra; Neptune and the Sun

BROTHERHOOD IS A WORK OF THE LIGHT

Carry the light of the Master's love into the world. You have come to earth for a special purpose; you have come not only to develop divine consciousness but to pioneer the pathway which will become the path for all who follow.

THE CHURCH or religion of the new age of Aquarius will be the religion of brotherhood, when old forms will be swept away.

YOU WILL never find a true teacher making big claims. A true teacher will understate rather than overstate. True teachers will be very careful about what they say, and you will always notice a quality of love, humility, gentleness, in their conversation.

WE ARE preaching a gospel of perfection; we know this very well, but then you have the seeds of perfection already in you!

Develop the consciousness of the Great White Light or the Christ within yourself. Not in the brow, but in your heart, and in the thousand-petalled lotus at the apex of your triangle. Work always with this higher triangle, and the Star.

WOULD that we could find words with which to describe the glory of the form of the master soul! We can give you perhaps an inkling of that glory by describing the form as appearing like a jewel. Think of a jewel casket; then open your casket, and lying upon a soft cushion see a golden jewel flashing like fire, dazzlingly beautiful. Rays from this jewel go in all directions.

WE SEE a world made beautiful. We see cities built not only with material substance, but beautified by the light of the spirit, and this spiritual power harnessed to physical and material needs. We see graceful and spacious buildings, with light radiating from the walls of the room, from the ceilings, although there seems to be no one particular point from which the light shines. More beautiful music will stimulate the mental qualities and will gently open the heart centre. That music is coming, and will raise the vibrations of the earth. Music is itself beautiful architecture.

YOU YOURSELF ARE THE TEMPLE

St John gave a description of the New Jerusalem, of the Golden City paved with gold, the gates decorated with blazing jewels. What is this but a portrayal of your own inner self?—your form the temple, your chakras the gates studded with beautiful jewels, your heart the throne upon which the King and Queen rest.

YOU yourself are the temple within the city of God; you are yourself the perfect cube, perfected through experience and perhaps through suffering, but at all events through your human relationships.

ALL ARE THE SAME IN GOD'S SIGHT

It does not matter very much who is a great soul and who is a young soul. We do not think it matters at all. Do not worship one whom you think is great, but endeavour to love all, both great and small, young and old. Love them all. All are the same in God's sight.

YOU ARE pioneers. You are given an opportunity to help the younger brethren onward and upward to the golden heights. As you walk the earth life, you are being guided and inspired and illumined by beings who now come to arouse and help humanity to go forth into the sunlight. May you all find happiness, serenity and a steady certainty.

EVERY DEATH IS A BIRTH

You do not enter upon eternal life until the full consciousness of the Christ life is born in you, until you have developed your solar body. Do you not see in the death of the physical body the great promise of the coming of the solar being, the solar body? Of course the lower aspect dies; but that supreme solar body which is being brought into being is leading you eventually to eternal life.

WHEN WE said that there would be a new planet born from the heart of the Sun or Son, we meant that from every life will be born a new world. This is beyond your comprehension at present, perhaps, but remember that you are all sons and daughters of God, and will become gods, from each of whom will be born a new world.

THE PHOENIX is representative of the initiate, or the one who dies to the lower self and is reborn in the higher self or in the spirit; and the eagle is representative of the Word of God, which descended from the heavens and was clothed in flesh. The divine Word lies within the innermost of every son and every daughter of God.

THE LANGUAGE OF THE MASTER

Do not try to put labels on people, and do not create idols of people, personalities. It seems to us that as soon as you confine the radiance of a spiritual being in a personality and you label him or her with a certain name, you are robbing that being of its true greatness, greatness which cannot be confined or limited to a human personality.

NO MASTER, we repeat, will contradict another: masters do not give essentially different teaching. They do not vary; they speak always the same language—not the language of any one particular country, but the language of the spirit, the language of love.

BE VERY universal in your thought regarding the masters. Think of them as one, and when you have found that *one,* you will see all, and in all you will see the one.

AS A SYMBOL of the new age, the white eagle soars into the heavens and sees far and wide.

$$\widehat{7}$$

THE MASTER soul, we repeat, is the gentle soul, the wise, loving and compassionate soul, patient in adversity, who never loses faith in God and the ministering angels.

THE GREATEST TREASURE

Let us gaze upon the perfect form of an Elder Brother—a master. What is the impression made upon us as we gaze upon that perfect form? Oh, such gentleness, such sweetness, such love! Can you conceive the purity and loveliness of the master soul? Can you see the expression, shining with love—not weak or tepid—a love which can withhold as well as give? Now, hold this picture ... feel the wisdom, the tenderness, the gentleness of the Mother, together with the strength, the power, the courage of the First Principle, the Father. See therefore the dual soul, and see this soul with power to watch over all human kind. Almost impossible as it is for the human mind to grasp, we would indeed endeavour to convey to you this sense of loving care in which you live and have your being.

THE MASTER is nearer than breathing, closer than hands and feet. This is simple truth. You will find nothing more beautiful than what you can find in your own inner temple. You will find there the greatest treasure, the perfect gift.

THE WHITE EAGLE PUBLISHING TRUST, which publishes and distributes the White Eagle teaching, is part of the wider work of the White Eagle Lodge, a meeting place or fraternity in which people may find a place for growth and understanding, and a place in which the teachings of White Eagle find practical expression. Here men and women may come to learn the reason for their life on earth and how to serve and live in harmony with the whole brotherhood of life, visible and invisible, in health and happiness. The White Eagle Publishing Trust website is at www.whiteaglepublishing.org.

Readers wishing to know more of the work of the White Eagle Lodge may write to the General Secretary, The White Eagle Lodge, New Lands, Brewells Lane, Liss, Hampshire, England GU33 7HY (tel. 01730 893300) or can call at The White Eagle Lodge, 9 St Mary Abbots Place, Kensington, London W8 6LS (tel. 020-7603 7914). In the Americas please write to The Church of the White Eagle Lodge, P. O. Box 930, Montgomery, Texas 77356 (tel. 936-597 5757), and in Australasia to The White Eagle Lodge (Australasia), P. O. Box 225, Maleny, Queensland 4552, Australia (tel. 07 5494 4397).

You can also visit our websites at

www.whiteagle.org (*worldwide*);
www.whiteaglelodge.org (*Americas*);
www.whiteeaglelodge.org.au (*Australasia*),

and you can email us at one of the addresses below.

enquiries@whiteagle.org (*worldwide*);
sjrc@whiteaglelodge.org (*Americas*);
enquiries@whiteeaglelodge.org.au (*Australasia*).